What's on Your Mind?

Why are you interested in a workbook on leadership?

Are you new to a leadership role and looking for a practical starting point? Are you having issues at work that you think might be addressed by developing your own leadership skills? Are you interested in something to develop emerging leaders in your organization?

Whatever your needs, take a moment to write it down here, now.
Don't skip this—it's important to articulate your thoughts before you begin.

I am concerned about: ________________________   I am interested in: ________________________
____________________________________   ____________________________________
____________________________________   ____________________________________
____________________________________   ____________________________________
____________________________________   ____________________________________
____________________________________   ____________________________________
____________________________________   ____________________________________
____________________________________   ____________________________________
____________________________________   ____________________________________
____________________________________   ____________________________________
____________________________________   ____________________________________
____________________________________   ____________________________________
____________________________________   ____________________________________

Introduction

The U.S. Small Business Administration defines a "small" business as anything from 1 to 500 employees. But an organization with 500 people functions quite differently from one with 12 or fewer – which are better described as "micro-organizations" (MOs). MOs make up an estimated 90% or more of all U.S. businesses and non-profits.

MOs face unique leadership challenges since they characteristically have limited resources of time, money and people. Many have an owner or leader participating in the work alongside everyone else in addition to trying to run the organization. Consequently, leaders of MOs are often too busy getting the work done to think much about how to improve their own performance as a leader. And even if they were interested in growing as a leader, not many leadership programs understand MOs' unique circumstances and constraints.

This program was designed for leaders who don't have time to wade through reams of information or compare leadership models trying to find something that helps; leaders who need something simple and practical – basic enough to be useful from day one, but also robust enough to serve as their organization grows. The purpose of this workbook is act as a compass today, while laying a solid foundation for the future.

What this workbook provides:

1. A look at why leadership matters even in a very small organization.

2. A concise explanation of D.A.M. Leadership's approach and how it can have an immediate impact on your organization, as well as guide you in the future.

3. A deeper dive into the three aspects of the framework (Direct, Align, & Manage) with worksheets to help you think through your specific situation.

4. A set of tools to help your personal, professional and leadership development:

   - *Self-Assessment*

   - *Self-Assessment Review*

   - *Employee Feedback*

   - *Feedback Assessment*

   - *Job Description Sample & Blank Form*

   - *A "SCOT" Review*

   - *30-60-90 Day Action Plan Sample & Blank Form*

Now, let's not waste one D.A.M. minute!

Why Leadership Matters for Micro-Organizations

Many people are in charge, but not many have prepared for it. Most people lead from a combination of imitating (or avoiding) what they've experience under other leaders, combined with their personality preferences and simple trial-and-error. But even those blessed with innate leadership ability rarely have a framework to maximize their results, identify their deficits, or effectively develop other leaders.

And why does leadership matter in a Micro-Organization (MO) anyway? After all, there's only a handful of people in the organization. Doesn't everyone know what they need to do? In a five-person non-profit, or a four-person software company, or an eight-person brewery, why bother with leadership development at all?

Because being in charge isn't the same thing as being a leader.

Anybody can start an organization and be a boss. Being in charge takes no special talent or training, and does not require competence.

A good leader is more than just a boss. Effective leaders create a healthy work environment and find fulfillment in doing so. They develop people while building high-functioning organizations that outperform the competition and reach their goals. They are intentional and engaged — they are needed. If you manage, direct or supervise any number of people, you are a leader and should take that responsibility seriously.

Because "shooting from the hip" is not a sustainable plan.

In most MOs, people wear a lot of hats including the leader(s); relationships can be hard to define; getting the work done takes priority over all else. There's often very little time to plan, meet, and discuss challenges and opportunities. And even when those meetings do occur, they're often not documented, and follow up is rare. It's the old cliche: *Too busy working <u>in</u> the business, to work <u>on</u> the business.*

The leader of an MO can't afford to remain reactive, always playing defense; always shooting from the hip. That method might work for a while but not over the long haul. Effective leaders are intentional; they play offense as well as defense.

Because working relationships are more critical the smaller the organization.

In a five-person salon, when one stylist calls in sick the company loses 20% of its workforce that day. Similarly, hiring one additional person has the potential to impact every single established relationship in the organization. Selecting the right people is important, and MOs don't always have a large pool of candidates to select from. Sometimes leaders who come on board an existing MO find themselves with "inherited" employees—some of those folks may need to go, and some may be too valuable to lose.

Leaders have to manage the work, but also the relationships that support the work.

Because you're probably frustrated by things you could fix if you knew how.

Making assumptions can be a source of serious problems for leaders in any size business, but it's a particular danger for MOs. *We all know what we do here, right? We all know what our role is here, right?* Assuming everyone is informed, on board, accountable, and prepared can lead to some ugly surprises. People can't be held accountable if they don't know what they are responsible for.

Good leaders know clarity can avoid frustration. They take the initiative to establish expectations, foster meaningful communication, and address the underlying issues of a problem, not merely its symptoms.

Because consequences in MOs are amplified.

Large organizations are often carried along by scale and sheer momentum when hit with adverse situations. Most MOs on the other hand don't have that luxury. Financial resources are usually tighter so cash flow is always a concern, and cash reserves (if any) can be eaten up quickly. Losing a valuable employee or client might make the difference to the annual success of an MO, or even its survival.

MOs need good leaders to minimize the impact of the challenges that larger organizations can weather more easily.

Because you're probably missing out on new opportunities.

MOs are normally busy getting the work done, but being busy can often be mistaken for success. While things are humming along, someone needs to be looking ahead to identify new trends, patterns and opportunities.

Good leaders keep their eyes open, not just to keep the organization on track, but to identify ways to grow and enhance the organization.

An Immediately Useful Leadership Framework

All that most leaders need to make an impact is a simple set of tools; an approach that is useful at every stage of their organization's development. That's the point of D.A.M. Leadership. Evaluating, identifying and taking action is the ongoing responsibility of a leader, not a one-time task. D.A.M. Leadership serves as a diagnostic tool for current issues but also a compass to plan your next steps. It's practical, scalable and teachable.

D.A.M. Leadership helps you to:
1. assess your situation,
2. address the issues you identify, and
3. bring structure that promotes growth.

Foundational to the D.A.M. Framework are two critical themes: ***intentionality*** and ***clarity***. These aren't character traits, they are choices and, hopefully, they'll become habits.

Intentionality means you do things on purpose, not accidentally or coincidentally. In leadership it means you accept the responsibility to guide your organization, your operations, and your people, and that you are willing to grow as a leader. Intentionality means taking time to think, plan, communicate, train, encourage, coach, assess, and report; you are committing to taking action and causing good things to happen.

Clarity means taking as many assumptions and as much guesswork out of a situation as possible. Ignorance and confusion can be cured by clarity. Clarity doesn't require unique wisdom or insight, it just requires simplification. Clarity begins by stating the obvious, often in writing. It also includes engaging your people and asking questions to see whether clarity has been achieved.

Clarity is the basis of accountability. You have no right to hold someone accountable for something they didn't know to do, or how it was to be done. A lack of clarity will inevitably lead to speculation, frustration, poor performance and possibly conflict. There's no excuse for lacking clarity in an MO. It's too easy and too important.

As you apply D.A.M. Leadership, you'll see how its three categories support each other and work together. These categories aren't rigid, they're complementary. Consequently, some of the subjects and practices in one area will overlap another.

The three essential actions of leadership—Direct, Align and Manage—will apply to your organization in ***three arenas***. The worksheet questions will help guide your thinking about how to Direct, Align and Manage…

1. the **Organization** itself,
2. the **Operations** of the organization, and
3. the **People** that make it all work.

Some aspects of this program will be more relevant than others depending on your unique set of circumstances and that's to be expected. Use the D.A.M. Leadership Worksheets as a diagnostic tool to discover what applies most in your current situation. You may find several areas that need to be addressed, but don't get overwhelmed—we've provided tools and resources to help you prioritize your actions.

Remember that even small changes can have big consequence; the main thing it to start somewhere. Be intentional, methodical and patient.

DIRECT

S ome leadership programs start by having you ask, ***Why do we exist?*** The answer to that question is then used to lay the foundation for a Mission or Vision Statement, which in turn presumably inspires people and drives the organization forward.

But for many MOs that's an academic exercise that doesn't really make much of a difference. A mission statement might make a great poster in the break room, but rarely helps to address the concerns that leaders of MOs face: problems of traction, performance and growth; sales and finances; retaining, motivating, and recruiting people. There are more useful questions to ask.

With that in mind, setting the direction of (and within) an MO will be about establishing a structure that everyone understands and can function in. It's about choices and communication to get people on the same page. To that end…

- **What do we do?**
- **What are our real values?**
- **What are our goals?**
- **What is the tone of our organization, that is, our culture?**

Building/creating/refining the direction of your organization should be collaborative whenever possible. As the leader, you have the right to direct everything and to make all the decisions. But that comes with consequences. Collaboration generates buy-in and a sense of ownership in the direction. That can be highly motivating. If people are self-motivated and engaged, then half your job is done! Your main responsibility will be deciding who is involved in creating or developing the direction of your organization. It isn't a democracy, but it should work as a team.

One important note about your MO's direction: it needs to be reviewed regularly to remain relevant—it can grow stale or dateed—but it shouldn't change too frequently since that becomes confusing.

WHAT DO WE DO?

Far too many MOs function on assumptions. Assumptions are cured by clarity. To gain clarity, your organization's purpose and activities should be in writing and as detailed as necessary. But don't try to reduce what your organization does to a single sentence like a Mission Statement. You should be able to explain your operations and activities in concrete, specific terms and avoid conceptual language. This will be the basis for other clarifying documents to follow for individuals and teams.

WHAT ARE OUR VALUES?

What guides any organization are its values—or more specifically, its *functional values*. Those are the genuine values that are active and noticeable in your organization, not a list of generic ideals like Integrity or Quality. Functional values are those that translate into real decisions, and they derive from the behavior of leadership, simple as that. Functional values guide daily operations and interactions with co-workers, suppliers and customers. From functional values flow standards, expectations, habits and ultimately the organization's culture.

If Customer Experience is truly one of your core values and not just a cliche you will make decisions based on long-term customer retention. If you value efficiency then you will consistently look for ways to improve your processes and cut waste. If a healthy workplace is important, then you will put effort toward creating an environment of trust and collaboration. Other functional values might include:

Productivity	**Creativity**	**Innovation**
Friendliness	**Orderliness**	**Communication**
Professionalism	**Proactivity**	**Sales**
Positivity	**Initiative**	**Excellence**
Fun	**Tradition**	**Profitability**
Camaraderie	**Enthusiasm**	**Winning**

[Note: Functional values are not always positive. If you don't mind cutting corners, or think your employees are beneath you, or place the bottom line above all else, those behaviors will show up in your decision-making—and set the tone for your organization.]

Leaders live out their functional values every single day. So, it's critical to define and model positive functional values since in MOs it's impossible to hide who you are for long.

WHAT ARE OUR GOALS?

Results are the product of setting, communicating and working toward clear goals. The old saying is true: *If you aim at nothing, you'll hit it every time.* Goals do not have to be "big and audacious" as some have suggested. They just need to be clear, attainable, and measurable. You may have more than one goal, but be realistic about the effort each will take so you don't overload your people or tax your resources.

Everyone from top to bottom should understand the goals of the organization. Thus, as the leader, it falls to you to communicate and clarify them as often as needed.

WHAT IS OUR CULTURE?

Values are the lines that mark the road, while culture (or tone) is how you drive that road. Culture is the organizational personality reflected in how you go about your business.

The attitude that permeates an organization can be implied or explicit, and it derives from the behavior of its leader(s). Whether you are efficient, demanding, easy-going, collaborative, introverted, anxious, etc. it will become part of the culture.

If you want to change the organization's culture, you will have to set a new tone. If you want it to feel like a family, you'll have to be intentional about it; if you want an atmosphere of innovation, you will have to model that. If you want a highly professional environment, it must start with you. Your behavior as a leader will be multiplied and followed, and that determines culture.

NOTES

DIRECT

This is a survey to help you set your leadership priorities. Some questions will be more relevant than others depending on your situation. Focus on what resonates but try to answer every question in some manner. Remember, you're working to improve your organization so it's important to document your efforts. When you answer these questions again in a few months you'll see where you've made progress, and what to focus on next.

1. What do we do?	2. What does success look like?
ORGANIZATION: Describe your organization in simple terms: its business, its approach, and its goals.	**ORGANIZATION:** Make a list of things that would demonstrate to you that your organization is succeeding.
OPERATIONS: Compile a list of the most basic operations (or activities) from your organization's description above.	**OPERATIONS:** For each operation, describe how you and others will know if they are working.
PEOPLE: List the positions in your organization. If you have teams, list them by name.	**PEOPLE:** Who needs to be involved in defining success, or setting direction for the operations or organization?

1. What do we do? (CONT.)	2. What does success look like? (CONT.)
ORGANIZATION:	**ORGANIZATION:**
OPERATIONS:	**OPERATIONS:**
PEOPLE:	**PEOPLE:**

DIRECT

This is a survey to help you set your leadership priorities. Some questions will be more relevant than others depending on your situation. Focus on what resonates but try to answer every question in some manner. Remember, you're working to improve your organization so it's important to document your efforts. When you answer these questions again in a few months you'll see where you've made progress, and what to focus on next.

3. What factors are essential to success?	4. What is the time frame?
ORGANIZATION: List things that are necessary for the organization to succeed (sales, specialized personnel, contracts, compliance, inventory, etc.)	**ORGANIZATION:** Review your essential success factors and note those that have a time constraint (daily, weekly, monthly, etc.)
OPERATIONS: List all essential activities or processes that keep things moving (website, response time, marketing, etc.)	**OPERATIONS:** Add any time constraints or schedules to the list of activities necessary for operations to succeed.
PEOPLE: List the most important tasks, requirements, and goals of each position (or team) from Question 1, under "People".	**PEOPLE:** List any schedule or deadline associated with the work of each job description, or team.

3. What factors are essential? (CONT.)	4. What is the time frame? (CONT.)
ORGANIZATION:	**ORGANIZATION:**
OPERATIONS:	**OPERATIONS:**
PEOPLE:	**PEOPLE:**

DIRECT

This is a survey to help you set your leadership priorities. Some questions will be more relevant than others depending on your situation. Focus on what resonates but try to answer every question in some manner. Remember, you're working to improve your organization so it's important to document your efforts. When you answer these questions again in a few months you'll see where you've made progress, and what to focus on next.

5. What are our Functional Values?	6. What is the culture of our organization?
ORGANIZATION: List the standards the organization actually lives and works by – those things that actually drive behavior.	Describe the culture (or tone) of your organization as it is today. Then note what elements you would like it to have going forward.
OPERATIONS: Detail the specific values that an operation needs to succeed (accuracy, timeliness, compliance, reporting, efficiency rating, etc.)	
PEOPLE: Detail the specific characteristics each role must demonstrate that are unique (polite, patient, responsive, thorough, etc.).	

5. What are our Functional Values? (CONT.)	6. What is the culture of our organization? (CONT.)
ORGANIZATION: **OPERATIONS:** **PEOPLE:**	

ALIGN

Once the direction of the organization is clear, alignment is simply making sure the resources are in place to get the job done. It largely answers the *How* question so that people can succeed in their individual roles, teams can function in their tasks, and the organization can reach its goals. Aligning various resources depends entirely on what the direction is. It's the difference between packing for the beach or the mountains.

Aligning, as with directing, should be as collaborative as possible. Those who are closest to the work often have insights that are valuable to improvement and innovation. Conversely, those who are somewhat removed might provide a fresh perspective that helps an operation or procedure become more efficient. You don't need input from everyone—too much feedback can slow decision-making. But as the leader you should be gathering well-informed and constructive feedback at every opportunity before making the final call.

The main elements of aligning your organization are...

- **Selecting and assigning**
- **Systems and processes**
- **Allocating resources**

SELECTING and ASSIGNING

Having the right people in the right position is a major key to success. The wrong person in a critical role is like trying to roll a stone uphill. This is why detailed, written job descriptions are so important. How will you know who's the best fit for a job without knowing what that job requires? From the top to the bottom, you have to identify the tasks that are essential to the function of the organization, and make them part of a job description. Then you have to match the best person to each role. Sounds simple, but in reality MOs don't always have a lot of people to choose from, and the people they have often wear a lot of hats. Additionally, very few people are "A-students" in all areas. But just like school, to move ahead a person needs a minimum level of competence in all subjects. The goal should be to maximize each person's performance by aligning them with jobs and tasks that fit their strengths while maintaining an acceptable level of performance in weaker areas.

Understanding how a person's skills and talents fit a role is just the beginning. Temperament, attitude, moral compass—even personal and family issues—can affect performance on the job. No one is a perfect match to any role, but the more factors you consider, the better your chances are to assign critical tasks to the right people.

SYSTEMS & PROCESSES

Organizations cannot function without systems and processes—order and routine keep things moving. The question for leaders is: Do we have the right systems and processes in place to succeed? It's a leader's responsibility to determine whether to create, refine, or eliminate systems and processes to keep working efficiently. Well-defined procedures keep people from shooting from the hip, reduce errors, and create predictable results. Does every procedure in your organization help your people succeed? Sometimes it's not the lack of procedures but too many that create inefficiency. A failure to perform may be due to burdensome or outdated systems: old software, cumbersome reporting, too many steps to access resources, etc.

The direction of the organization should determine the systems and processes. Routine procedures can set people free from re-inventing the wheel. But remember, systems should empower people, not eliminate thinking or personal initiative. The functional values you define when setting the direction will be useful in keeping procedures from becoming confused with the goal itself. Procedures are a means to an end.

ALLOCATING RESOURCES

There are essential tools for every job without which the work either cannot be done, or cannot be done efficiently. Three carpenters framing a house all need hammers, but they probably don't need three trucks. Resources can be tangible things like a laptop, power tools, software, etc. or less obvious like staging space, a payroll service, or a customer follow-up program. Some items are resources for individuals and some for the organization as a whole. Money, is often the most misunderstood resource in an MO. Budgets may or may not exist; individuals may have the authority to spend within certain limits, or they may have to ask for every dime they need. Accounting is more than totaling up dollars coming in and going out, it's a means of supporting the direction you want to the organization to go.

As critical as finances can be, an equally important resource to consider is time. Time is limited for everyone, so how it's allocated is crucial. Generally speaking, the longer something takes, the more it costs. When time is viewed as the valuable resource that it is, scheduling becomes a critical success factor for MOs. All tasks can be viewed as either concurrent or consecutive. Concurrent operations can be done at the same time since neither operation is dependent on the other. You can clean your tools while the concrete sets; you can answer emails while your report prints out. Consecutive operations require tasks to occur in a specific order. You can't install new carpet until the ceiling is painted; you can't turn the water back on until the faucet is replaced. Understanding the distinction between concurrent and consecutive activities can maximize efficiency and avoid bottlenecks.

As a leader, you need to provide the resources necessary for each job to be successful, without spreading those resources too thin. This means prioritizing activities and tracking results. Here again, clarity is vital.

ALIGN

This is a survey to help you set your leadership priorities. Some questions will be more relevant than others depending on your situation. Focus on what resonates but try to answer every question in some manner. Remember, you're working to improve your organization so it's important to document your efforts. When you answer these questions again in a few months you'll see where you've made progress, and what to focus on next.

1. Is everything aligned to support our purpose, and the goals we've defined?	2. What resources do we already have in place to succeed?
ORGANIZATION: Are you doing anything that is unnecessary or a distraction to your purpose? Are any of your goals in conflict or competition with each other?	**ORGANIZATION:** List all resources that support the organization that are up and running (location, equipment, people, finances, sales and marketing, etc.)
OPERATIONS: Assess all the practices of the organization to see if they support your goals. Note which should be reconsidered.	**OPERATIONS:** Describe the elements that support each specific operation, including the names of the people involved, procedures, budgets, tools, training, etc.
PEOPLE: Do all your people have a current written job description that they understand? If not, what roles need one?	**PEOPLE:** List the people involved in essential operations and each one's strengths as it applies to their role.

1. Is everything aligned to support our purpose, and the goals we've defined? (CONT.)	2. What resources do we already have in place to succeed? (CONT.)
ORGANIZATION:	**ORGANIZATION:**
OPERATIONS:	**OPERATIONS:**
PEOPLE:	**PEOPLE:**

ALIGN

This is a survey to help you set your leadership priorities. Some questions will be more relevant than others depending on your situation. Focus on what resonates but try to answer every question in some manner. Remember, you're working to improve your organization so it's important to document your efforts. When you answer these questions again in a few months you'll see where you've made progress, and what to focus on next.

3. What resources are we missing or would like to have?	4. Is there an alignment of attitude within the organization?
ORGANIZATION: Is there any resource that you are missing that would enhance your success?	**ORGANIZATION:** How confident are you that the organization is on the right track? Do your people believe in the organization?
OPERATIONS: Is there any operation or procedure that could be added to improve the organization?	**OPERATIONS:** Are people being asked to function under systems or routines that outdated or cumbersome? Are there any personnel issues that could be addressed by changes to an operation or procedure?
PEOPLE: How well do your people fit for their current roles? Is there anyone who needs more training? Do tasks or roles need to be reassigned for a better fit? Are there open positions?	**PEOPLE:** Does everyone, including you, understand and embrace their roles? Do teams function to their fullest? Is there any reluctance or push back by anyone?

<table>
<tr>
<td></td>
<td></td>
</tr>
<tr>
<td>ORGANIZATION:</td>
<td>ORGANIZATION:</td>
</tr>
<tr>
<td>OPERATIONS:</td>
<td>OPERATIONS:</td>
</tr>
<tr>
<td>PEOPLE:</td>
<td>PEOPLE:</td>
</tr>
</table>

ALIGN

This is a survey to help you set your leadership priorities. Some questions will be more relevant than others depending on your situation. Focus on what resonates but try to answer every question in some manner. Remember, you're working to improve your organization so it's important to document your efforts. When you answer these questions again in a few months you'll see where you've made progress, and what to focus on next.

5. Are we supporting the culture we say we want?

Review the list of elements that you want to be part of the Culture (question 6 from the DIRECT worksheet), and then note what resources, practices, habits and programs you have in place to support and encourage those characteristics to grow. Is there anything more you can do?

MANAGE

Managing combines direction and alignment—keeping the people, the systems and the resources you've put in place working together to achieve results. It includes monitoring, overseeing, staying on schedule, problem-solving, reporting and evaluating. And since people are involved, people-skills are very helpful for a leader. Treating people well isn't just the right thing to do, it's the smart thing to do. In an MO, each person represents a significant percentage of the whole workforce, so even one individual who's absent, unengaged, or disruptive can have a big impact on the organization as a whole.

Managing includes learning what motivates each one of your people and developing those who show potential and want to grow; handling resistance to change and interpersonal conflicts with objectivity; addressing failure to comply with agreed upon standards in a constructive manner. Managing is about building trust.

Trust is a by-product of your behavior. Being consistently respectful, applying the same standards to yourself as to your people, accepting feedback and being approachable, keeping your word—all these work to develop trust. Trust creates buy-in and motivates people to go beyond what is asked of them.

Good people-leaders know that camaraderie is very important but that an objective distance is equally important. It's great to have fun together and go out socially once in a while but what happens when you have to turn someone down for a raise? Or tell them they can't take a day off? MOs are particularly susceptible to blurred relationships, thus maintaining objectivity with your people is foundational to managing well. Objectivity means seeing things and people as they really are so you can make sound decisions without undue influences. For example, if someone you really like is creating a problem, you can't overlook it; if someone you find annoying is right about an issue, you should listen. If you have relatives in your organization, you can't treat them differently than the others.

Objectivity applies to yourself as well. If you aren't good at leading meetings, let someone else lead them. If you're holding onto an outdated practice simply because you like it, you need to let it go. Maintaining an objective view of the organization, its progress, its people—and yourself—is how good leaders manage successfully. Don't let ego or insecurity drive your leadership.

Here are the four categories to focus on when managing:

- **Clarify and train**
- **Motivate and develop**
- **Build effective teams**
- **Measure and review**

CLARIFY & TRAIN

Clarity is about developing proper expectations, which becomes the basis for accountability. You can't hold someone responsible for what they didn't know they were supposed to do. Clarity begins with the first two steps of D.A.M. Leadership: directing and aligning. The more thorough you are in those categories the easier managing expectations will be. Nevertheless, there will always be variables and so it's nearly impossible to *over*-clarify since even your best people can be distracted, confused, or overwhelmed. If in doubt, state the obvious, reinforce the basics, and repeat yourself without apology.

Think of training as a deep and focused form of clarity—something that will remove all questions about how to perform a specific task or function in a given role. Training allows people to succeed and drives the organization forward. It may include instructions on strict safety protocols that cannot be compromised or involve *soft* skills like customer service that rely less on rigid compliance than on interpersonal expertise. Whatever the need of the role, the training should address and support it.

MOTIVATE & DEVELOP

Even though leading people takes work, the good news is most people want to do a good job. They like to feel that their work matters and that it's noticed. Nothing motivates like be appreciated. As one writer put it, *Catch someone doing something right*. Positive reinforcement is always welcome, as long as it's sincere and informed—you can't just slap people on the back and think that's enough.

Keep in mind that not everyone is motivated by the same things. One will work harder for a bonus, another for time off, and another for public recognition. Certainly, all potential rewards will motivate to some degree, but it's important to know that all people aren't wired identically.

Developing people can be divided into three categories: *professional*, *personal* and *leadership*.

Professional development is simply helping people grow in their work skills and advance their career. Everyone learns better under the yoke of responsibility, so for those who want to develop professionally, new challenges, assignments and opportunities will be essential.

Personal development can be tricky because people do not always see their need to change. It takes a certain amount of maturity and self-awareness for someone to develop personally, and there may be resistance. In the workplace, some personal development will take place as people function in teams, set and reach goals, work under a deadline, etc. Keep in mind though that the workplace has its limitations when it comes to personal development and thus it should not be your main goal.

Leadership development can be as easy as putting someone in charge of a one-time project or as involved as training your successor. But in all cases, it should be reserved for the ones who really want it; as you already know, leading can be a tough job. Don't worry about "natural leadership ability"—which is great but not necessary. What's essential is a desire to lead and a willingness to learn. Just remember, you have a limited amount of time and energy so select carefully who you will pour your efforts into as a leader.

BUILD EFFECTIVE TEAMS

History tells us that while a single person can do a great deal of damage, almost nothing of lasting value has ever been achieved without teamwork.

Depending on the size of your MO, you may have only one team—the entire organization itself! But even an organization of two people needs to understand the fundamentals of teamwork. Like an equally matched pair of oxen, you must pull in the same direction and with the same effort. If you have more than a handful of folks then you may have multiple teams, and how teams interact with other teams is as important as how individuals interact with other individuals.

Teams are an easy concept to grasp, but not always an easy one to implement. Most MOs create teams from a very limited pool of candidates. That means you might have to compose a team with less-than-ideal individuals, and some people could be on multiple teams. You will have to be honest about the strengths and weaknesses of the teams you compose and modify your expectations concerning their collective abilities and competing demands.

Effective teams, despite any inherent limits, all function based on well-established standards: Clearly defined roles, a common goal, good communication and above all, trust. Trust, as mentioned earlier, is a byproduct and comes only as people respect each other and keep their word.

MEASURE & REVIEW

The old saying is true: *What gets measured, gets managed*. The most important thing to measure for an organization of any size is its finances. Obviously the purpose of a business is to make money, but even non-profits have to pay bills and meet payroll. Ignorance of finances and the lack a real budget is the fastest way to go out of business. How the money comes in and goes out is one of the primary responsibilities of the organization's top leader; you may have a CFO but you can't entirely delegate this critical metric.

Other aspects of an MO will need some form of measurement as well. What are your critical success factors? What will interrupt the work? What will lose customers? What will take you to the next level? Those are the kind of questions that need to be answered if you want to define what needs to be measured. From sales, to inventory, to online reviews—if you decide it's important to the health and survival of your MO, then it needs to be tracked.

Reporting, however, is pointless without understanding what the data is telling you and taking action. For example, if you track monthly sales and know that summer is a slow time, you can run a special in May to boost revenue, cut back on overtime, schedule more vacation hours, or a combination of things. The point of measuring and reviewing what you've measured is to take steps to avoid problems and identify opportunities.

People and teams also need some form of measurement, whether it's an annual review, quarterly reports, weekly time sheets, etc. If you've set the direction of the organization, and aligned the resources to support it, then you must develop some meaningful way to gauge your progress.

MANAGE

This is a survey to help you set your leadership priorities. Some questions will be more relevant than others depending on your situation. Focus on what resonates but try to answer every question in some manner. Remember, you're working to improve your organization so it's important to document your efforts. When you answer these questions again in a few months you'll see where you've made progress, and what to focus on next.

1. How are we doing?	2. What metrics or reports are in place to know whether we are on track?
ORGANIZATION: Grade your organization on how well you're fulfilling your purpose and/or reaching your goals. Note areas of concern.	**ORGANIZATION:** What tools do you have to show the progress of the organization as a whole? What financial reports do you use?
OPERATIONS: Are all the operations and procedures functioning efficiently? If not, what's missing? Who will address this? When?	**OPERATIONS:** What measurements or reports are in place to track essential operations? Who is responsible to determine if operations are working efficiently or need review?
PEOPLE: Are all your people clear on their role and responsibilities? Do any of them need more training in their current role?	**PEOPLE:** How are you gauging the performance of individuals and teams?

<table>
<tr><td>1. How are we doing? (CONT.)</td><td>2. What metrics or reports are in place to know whether we are on track? (CONT.)</td></tr>
<tr><td>ORGANIZATION:</td><td>ORGANIZATION:</td></tr>
<tr><td>OPERATIONS:</td><td>OPERATIONS:</td></tr>
<tr><td>PEOPLE:</td><td>PEOPLE:</td></tr>
</table>

MANAGE

This is a survey to help you set your leadership priorities. Some questions will be more relevant than others depending on your situation. Focus on what resonates but try to answer every question in some manner. Remember, you're working to improve your organization so it's important to document your efforts. When you answer these questions again in a few months you'll see where you've made progress, and what to focus on next.

3. How do we communicate?	4. What challenges, obstacles or conflicts are we facing?
ORGANIZATION: How do you update your people on the progress of the organization, or changes coming?	**ORGANIZATION:** Review your essential success factors and note anything that could, or does, interfere with them.
OPERATIONS: Do you have an employee handbook? Do you have meetings on any regular basis? How do you communicate changes in procedures to your people?	**OPERATIONS:** What obstacles exist that affect the performance of your operations? Are they internal or external?
PEOPLE: How does information get to each individual in the organization? Do you have a way for each person to respond?	**PEOPLE:** Is anyone not fully engaged, performing poorly, or causing unnecessary stress? Who will address those issues?

<table>
<tr><td>3. How do we communicate? (CONT.)</td><td>4. What challenges, obstacles or conflicts are we facing? (CONT.)</td></tr>
<tr><td>ORGANIZATION:</td><td>ORGANIZATION:</td></tr>
<tr><td>OPERATIONS:</td><td>OPERATIONS:</td></tr>
<tr><td>PEOPLE:</td><td>PEOPLE:</td></tr>
</table>

MANAGE

This is a survey to help you set your leadership priorities. Some questions will be more relevant than others depending on your situation. Focus on what resonates but try to answer every question in some manner. Remember, you're working to improve your organization so it's important to document your efforts. When you answer these questions again in a few months you'll see where you've made progress, and what to focus on next.

5. Are we intentionally motivating and developing our people?

ORGANIZATION:
What challenges or opportunities are available to help your people develop professionally or personally? Have you identified anyone for leadership development?

OPERATIONS:
What incentive programs or rewards are in place to motivate your people? How do you gauge the success of those programs?

PEOPLE:
List anyone who needs professional development, and what actions you can take.

6. How are we, as leaders, guiding and fostering the culture?

Ultimately, the behavior of leaders shapes the culture of an organization. What are you and your other leaders doing to reinforce and grow the culture of your organization?

5. Are we intentionally motivating and developing our people? (CONT.)	6. How are we, as leaders, guiding and fostering the culture? (CONT.)
ORGANIZATION:	
OPERATIONS:	
PEOPLE:	

Taking the Next D.A.M. Steps

Hopefully the preceding worksheets have helped you identify areas of both strengths and challenges (not *weaknesses*–that implies helplessness, and as an intentional leader you are never helpless).

Perhaps you've never thought in terms of leading in three arenas (Organization, Operations and People) and that's offered you some new insights. Maybe you've been able to clarify some issues that weren't well-defined. Now it's time to bring together the things you need to focus on. As mentioned before, you can't make too many changes at once, but you need to begin doing something. Use the summary below to record the most critical areas that you noted on the worksheets. They may or may not be related to each other and that's fine. What you fill in here will serve as a basis for your **30-60-90 Day Action Plan** found in the Appendix (p.59).

Use this form to identify the most critical issues you want address:

1. review your answers from the Direct, Align and Manage worksheets; note those responses that you feel the strongest about.
2. in each arena–Organization, Operations and People–summarize your thoughts, questions, concerns, or action items.

D.A.M. Summary *example*

DIRECT	ALIGN	MANAGE
ORGANIZATION: #3 – our success depends on inventory and that's been too low this year.	**ORGANIZATION:** #2 – our location and warehousing is fine, but we need stronger sales.	**ORGANIZATION:** #1 – I'd give us a B+ on fulfillment, and a C- on sales.
OPERATIONS: #3 – our software is out of date and that's impacting inventory tracking.	**OPERATIONS:** #1 – are we spread too thin? Are we trying to accommodate too many different kinds of clients?	**OPERATIONS:** #3 – an updated handbook and monthly production meetings would help our communication.
PEOPLE: #5 – we're lacking a sense of urgency in sales. There's not enough in the pipeline.	**PEOPLE:** #3 – Dave needs more training to manage the warehouse better.	**PEOPLE:** #3 – we need a way to get feedback/suggestions from everyone faster.

CULTURE:

We are a very quality-minded organization, and we have solid relationships internally. But we need to be more efficient — we need to value response time and communication more.

D.A.M. Summary

DIRECT	ALIGN	MANAGE
ORGANIZATION:	ORGANIZATION:	ORGANIZATION:
OPERATIONS:	OPERATIONS:	OPERATIONS:
PEOPLE:	PEOPLE:	PEOPLE:

CULTURE:

TOOLBOX

The following section provides simple, practical tools to help you grow as a leader, better engage your people, and to take action to improve your organization. You may want to make copies to work on, and to share with others in your organization.

Your Toolbox Includes:

1. Self-Assessment
Self-awareness is foundational to being an effective leader. This tool will help you evaluate areas that directly impact your leadership and therefore your organization.

2. Self-Assessment Review
The review is designed to coalesce your thoughts into actionable items.

3. Employee Feedback
Feedback is a useful tool for seeing things we might be missing – a few meaningful questions can save a lot of guesswork. Not all feedback is equally valuable; some perspectives will be more informed than others. Still, knowing how everyone in your organization feels is important.

4. Feedback Assessment
This form helps you organize the feedback you receive. Consider all feedback carefully whether it enlightens, confirms, or challenges you before putting action items into your plan.

5. Job Description (Example & Blank Form)
A written job description is a simple but often overlooked tool that can clarify expectations for everyone in the organization. Do not neglect to create one for your own role.

6. A "SCOT" Review (Example & Blank Form)
The SCOT Review helps identify the Strengths, Challenges, Opportunities and Threats that affect you currently, or might in the future. It's a great brainstorming tool for teams.

7. 30-60-90 Day Action Plan (Example & Blank Form)
Not much gets accomplished without a plan, and this tool helps you move steadily, and realistically, toward your goals. Over time, it will also become a record of your accomplishments.

Self-Assessment

We all have areas of **STRENGTH**, areas that **STRETCH** us, and areas that we **STRUGGLE** with. Answer as objectively as you can; it's for your own benefit.

Circle a number: **AGREE** .... **DISAGREE**

1. I understand my own values, attitudes and biases.	5 4 3 2 1
2. I can easily identify what emotions I am experiencing.	5 4 3 2 1
3. I pay attention to how my language and behavior impacts others.	5 4 3 2 1
4. I am able to maintain my composure in difficult or stressful situations.	5 4 3 2 1
5. I manage my impulses well and do not overreact to what others say or do.	5 4 3 2 1
6. I am trustworthy, and I follow through on my commitments.	5 4 3 2 1
7. I lead by example.	5 4 3 2 1
8. I accept responsibility for my actions and do not blame others.	5 4 3 2 1
9. I value people, and treat them with respect.	5 4 3 2 1
10. I listen to different points of view and consider opposing opinions.	5 4 3 2 1
11. I seek feedback from others, even if it might be negative.	5 4 3 2 1
12. I communicate clearly and effectively.	5 4 3 2 1
13. I am able to voice my opinion even if it might be an unpopular one.	5 4 3 2 1
14. I am comfortable giving praise and encouragement to others.	5 4 3 2 1
15. I am able to give honest feedback regardless of someone's reaction.	5 4 3 2 1
16. I manage conflict to create a positive outcome.	5 4 3 2 1
17. I can put myself in another's shoes and see things from their perspective.	5 4 3 2 1
18. I am able to laugh at myself and am not easily offended.	5 4 3 2 1
19. I give others the benefit of the doubt, rather than assuming the worst.	5 4 3 2 1
20. I understand what my role as a leader requires.	5 4 3 2 1
21. I actively work to improve my leadership skills.	5 4 3 2 1
22. I am able to motivate and influence people.	5 4 3 2 1
23. I balance my personal feelings toward people and view them objectively.	5 4 3 2 1
24. I am adaptable and can face challenges without becoming frustrated.	5 4 3 2 1
25. I do not procrastinate.	5 4 3 2 1
26. I am not easily distracted from my goals.	5 4 3 2 1
27. I can generally read the emotions of others without difficulty.	5 4 3 2 1
28. I am not anxious, impulsive or arbitrary in my decision-making.	5 4 3 2 1
29. I understand the professional goals and aspirations of my people.	5 4 3 2 1
30. I am committed to seeing my people succeed, develop and feel fulfilled.	5 4 3 2 1
31. I take time to reflect on my organization and plan for the future.	5 4 3 2 1
32. I am willing to make personal sacrifices to grow the organization.	5 4 3 2 1

Self-Assessment Review *part 1*

Addressing Areas of STRETCH & STRUGGLE	These are likely impacting your organization, whether you realize it or not.
Did you rate yourself on any question with a 1 or a 2? List those below.	*Acknowledging areas of struggle may be hard, but it might be the quickest way to identify critical areas affecting your organization.*
Are there patterns or themes that tie these areas together? (Perhaps not, or perhaps more than one.)	*Identifying patterns (ex. avoiding conflict, not controlling your emotions, etc.) can help direct your efforts more effectively.*
How do these issues show up in your leadership experience?	*A leader's behavior impacts everything. The good news is that your areas of weakness are probably your greatest opportunities for immediate improvement.*
Ask for feedback from trusted co-workers, friends, or mentors on these issues. Find out what they would suggest you stop doing (or start doing) to improve in these areas. Record key points here.	*We all need feedback to grow. Be open to comments or suggestions that can help you identify blind spots, or areas that need change, even if it's not offered in the way you would like it.*
ACTION ITEMS:	*List a few things you can do with the information you've learned. What would improve your leadership and benefit your organization the most? Keep your plan simple, and if applicable, put some reminders on your calendar to check on your progress.*

Self-Assessment Review *part 2*

Understanding Your STRENGTHS	*Effective leaders understand how to use their strengths correctly, and develop them further.*
Did you rate yourself on any question with a 5? List those below.	*Don't be modest. Good leaders generally have many strengths, and are highly self-aware.*
Are there patterns or themes that tie these areas together? (Perhaps not, or perhaps more than one.)	*Identifying patterns can help you understand more about your personal leadership style.*
How do these strong points show up in your leadership experience?	*Strengths are great, but they need to be utilized in a balanced fashion. It's easy to fall into a habit of doing only what you are good at or what you enjoy.*
Ask for feedback. Are you as strong in these areas as you think? Is there any tendency to "over use" your strengths? What strengths could be use more as a leader? Record key points here.	*Confirmation of your strengths is important. It means you aren't the only one who thinks you're doing a good job. It's also possible you aren't utilizing all your strengths to their fullest. Feedback can help you develop your strengths, not just face your weaknesses.*
NEXT STEPS:	*List a few things you can do with the information you've learned. Are you relying on your strengths enough? Do you need to balance them in some way? Keep your plan simple, and if applicable, put some reminders on your calendar.*

NOTES

DAM
DIRECT   ALIGN   MANAGE

Self-Assessment Review *part 3*

"Know Thyself"
– The Oracle of Delphi

Areas of **STRETCH** and **STRUGGLE** normally have some obvious impact on your leadership, and therefore your organization. They need to be faced openly, with a plan. It doesn't have to be a complex one but it needs to be specific. It might include delegating some critical tasks to someone whose strengths match the need; it might include training; it might be sharing your struggles with your team to get their perspective. The main point is that any shortcoming that impacts your leadership cannot be ignored without consequences.

STRENGTHS are easy to rely on and for good reason. Being adept at some aspects of leadership more than others is normal. Enjoy your strengths and look for ways to develop them. You might be able to go from *good* to *great* in some areas.

Be aware that strengths can also be over-utilized too. As the saying goes, *If all you have is a hammer, everything looks like a nail.* Your leadership challenges may not always fall in line with your strengths, and to assume they do means you might be addressing an issue with the wrong tools.

So, what about your **MIDDLE** scores? Simply put, anything that you rated a **3** or a **4** should be addressed only as needed. No one is all **5s** (and if rated yourself that way, you need to go back and be more honest with yourself!) Keep an eye on your middle scores: Don't let a **3** slip to a **2**. Evaluate your **4s** to see if you can improve them if it's worth the effort.

3s that I need to keep an eye on:

____
____
____
____
____
____
____

4s that I might be able to build on:

____
____
____
____
____
____
____

Employee Feedback

Circle a number: **AGREE** .... **DISAGREE**

	AGREE				DISAGREE
1. I understand my own role at work.	5	4	3	2	1
2. I can easily get clarification on things that come up.	5	4	3	2	1
3. My supervisor communicates clearly his/her expectations.	5	4	3	2	1
4. I am able to offer feedback to my supervisor even if it's not positive.	5	4	3	2	1
5. I have the tools and resources to do my job.	5	4	3	2	1
6. I am trusted to do my work without being micro-managed.	5	4	3	2	1
7. In the last month, I have received praise or recognition for doing a good job.	5	4	3	2	1
8. I feel like a valued member of the organization.	5	4	3	2	1
9. I am treated with respect.	5	4	3	2	1
10. My opinions are appreciated and taken seriously by my supervisor.	5	4	3	2	1
11. I believe my supervisor treats everyone fairly, and does not play favorites.	5	4	3	2	1
12. I feel comfortable asking questions about the organization's direction.	5	4	3	2	1
13. I understand and believe in the values of the organization.	5	4	3	2	1
14. I believe my organization is on the right track to succeed.	5	4	3	2	1
15. I am on good terms with my co-workers.	5	4	3	2	1
16. I believe my co-workers are committed to doing a good job.	5	4	3	2	1
17. As an organization, we handle conflict in a positive way.	5	4	3	2	1
18. My supervisor encourages me to grow in my career and develop new skills.	5	4	3	2	1
19. I feel like there is room for me to develop professionally in the organization.	5	4	3	2	1
20. I feel supported when a personal issue arises that affects my work.	5	4	3	2	1
21. My supervisor is concerned that I have a healthy work-life balance.	5	4	3	2	1

Are there things you would like your supervisor to **STOP** doing, **START** doing, or **KEEP** doing as a leader?

Use this opportunity to address specific actions or behaviors your supervisor should be aware of.

DAM
DIRECT ALIGN MANAGE

Feedback Assessment

CONSIDERING YOUR OPPORTUNITIES	*Positive or negative, feedback is an opportunity for a leader.*
What areas were rated a 1 or a 2 by your team? List those below.	*Not all negative ratings mean there's a real problem—but as a leader you should at least be aware of the feelings within your organization.*
Are there patterns or themes that tie these areas together? (Perhaps not, or perhaps more than one.)	*If you find similar low ratings from several responders, those areas should be investigated first. If more than one person pointed to the same issue, it's likely a real issue not just one person's opinion.*
Can you see any connection of these patterns to your own answers from your Self-Assessment?	*Employee feedback can confirm things you knew, or open your eyes to new things. The goal is personal and professional growth, even if it's uncomfortable.*
Confirm the accuracy of the feedback you've received with someone you trust, inside or outside the organization. Record key points here.	*Not all opinions are informed, balanced, or objective. Before you assume you need to change some area of your leadership consult with someone you trust to discuss it.*
ACTION ITEMS:	*List a few things you can do with the information you've learned. What would improve your leadership and benefit your organization the most? Keep your plan simple, and if applicable, put some reminders on your calendar to check on your progress.*

DAM

DIRECT | ALIGN | MANAGE

Job Description *example*

This is a tool to create clarity for both the employer and the employee. It's the foundation for success individually and organizationally and allows for accountability.

Title: Hair Stylist	Keep the job title simple and functional.
Reports to: Salon Manager, Jane Smith	The title and name of the person who will give directions, answer questions, etc. on a regular basis.
Functions: • Hair cutting & styling services for all ages; men and women • Hair coloring • Permanents • Appearance consultation	List basic bullet points that describe what the role involves. Some jobs may take more explanation than others, but try to keep these points as simple as possible.
Responsibilities: • Provide assigned services in a professional manner • Work days/hours agree upon unless approved • Book and manage clients independently using salon software • Comply with all hygiene procedures • Keep workspace and common areas clean • Answer incoming calls when receptionist is unavailable • Communicate safety issues promptly • Coordinate coverage for clients when absent unexpectedly • Maintain a professional appearance when at the salon • Assist Manager with general duties as requested • Maintain all state licensing and/or educational requirements	Responsibilities are those activities you expect people to do and for which they will be evaluated. This is an "actions" list that should clarify expectations and help your people succeed. This list can be as long and detailed as necessary. You can't hold someone accountable for what they did not know was their responsibility.
Requirements: • Fluent in English • Licensed in the state of _________ • 3+ years experience in a salon • Valid driver's license, or reliable transportation	Anything that is required to perform in the role effectively. Some of these may be flexible (like years of experience) and some may be mandatory (like government licensing).
Other Expectations: • Strong verbal communication skills • Positive attitude • Punctuality • Ability to follow instructions, verbal or written • Availability for occasional company social functions / events • Support other staff to create a positive workplace	This list will include things that apply to the culture of the organization, soft skills, and anything that will help avoid surprises on both sides.
Acknowledgment: I have reviewed and understand the above Job Description. I believe it to be accurate and complete, and that I can successfully fulfill each duty or task. I also agree that management retains the right to amend this Job Description at any time.	Signing the job description creates a sense of accountability. After signing, make a copy so that each of you will have a record.

_______________________________   ___________
Signature   Date

Job Description

Name ______________________________

NOTES:

Title:

Reports to:

Functions:

Responsibilities:

Requirements:

Other Expectations:

Acknowledgment:
I have reviewed and understand the above Job Description. I believe it to be accurate and complete, and that I can successfully fulfill each duty or task. I also agree that management retains the right to amend this Job Description at any time.

______________________________   ______________
Signature   Date

NOTES

DAM
DIRECT | ALIGN | MANAGE

SCOT Review *example*

A SCOT Review looks at your **S**trengths, **C**hallenges, **O**pportunities and **T**hreats. It's a tool to identify and evaluate issues that affect you currently, or might in the future. It's a great brainstorming tool for teams.

Date ____________

STRENGTHS
What does your organization consistently do well? What positions you to succeed in the future?

- Customer service
- We always follow up with our clients
- Our clients recommend us to others
- Our prices are competitive
- We have one of the best reputations in the area
- We've grown sales steadily for the last 3 years — strong sales staff
- Cash reserves are pretty good
- Solid relationship with our banker

CHALLENGES
What areas or issues are clearly interfering with your success or holding you back?

- Too much turn over in manufacturing; hard to retain experienced people
- Need to update our online presence to keep up with competition
- Internal communication could be much better, too many surprises
- Strained relationship with an important supplier

OPPORTUNITIES
What opportunities do you currently have that you'd like pursue? What opportunities would you like to investigate for the future?

- One more person on the floor could bring in considerably more sales
- Move locations would improve walk-in traffic
- If ABC competitor closes, we could pick up new clients as well as some of their people

THREATS
What threatens the well-being, success or survival of your organization?

- If Kelly's husband gets transferred we're gonna need to find someone fast
- XYZ competitor is targeting some of our people
- Road construction has impacted our walk-in traffic and online sales are not making up the difference
- Lease renewal in 18 months, expecting a substantial increase
- Suppliers becoming harder to find

SCOT Review

Be as specific as possible, and try to prioritize your answers so you can use what you learn for your Action Plan.

Date ______________

STRENGTHS
What does your organization consistently do well?
What positions you to succeed in the future?

CHALLENGES
What areas or issues are clearly interfering with your success or holding you back?

OPPORTUNITIES
What opportunities do you currently have that you'd like pursue? What opportunities would you like to investigate for the future?

THREATS
What threatens the well-being, success or survival of your organization?

NOTES

30 / 60 / 90 Day Action Plan *example*

This is a tool to keep you on track toward your goals. Nothing gets done without a deadline, but be realistic about the effort each item will take. The 30-Day column will normally have a longer list: some quick things, but also those that need to happen in order to reach your 60-Day and 90-Day goals.

30-Day Action Items

Complete by: Sept. 15

- Review all employees hired last year
- Advertise for receptionist position
  — update Job Description
  — Facebook and Instagram
  — investigate other on-line resources
- Mailer for open house
  — check postage costs
  — develop targeted mailing list
- organize inventory
  — John and Dave
  — Provide purchase orders and Invoices to match
- order and install new computer; begin training on accounting software

60-Day Action Items

Complete by: Oct. 15

- Review budget and decide on raises
- Complete all Interviews, make offer
  — set up schedule for training
  — set up goals for 30 days
- Design mailer with graphic artist
  — find a printer who handles mailing
  — mail and track

90-Day Action Items

Complete by: Nov. 15

- Complete 30 day review
- Review results with Diane and Sue

NOTES

DAM
DIRECT | ALIGN | MANAGE

30 / 60 / 90 Day Action Plan

This is a tool to keep you on track toward your goals. Nothing gets done without a deadline, but be realistic about the effort each item will take. The 30-Day column will normally have a longer list: some quick things, but also those that need to happen in order to reach your 60-Day and 90-Day goals.

Complete by: _______

90-Day Action Items

Complete by: _______

60-Day Action Items

Complete by: _______

30-Day Action Items

DAM

DIRECT | ALIGN | MANAGE

What's *Your* Plan?

Sometimes learning something new can *feel* like change, but it's not. Leaders make things happen. Leaders make choices. Leaders are intentional.

With what you've learned from this workbook, what will you, *as a leader*, commit to doing? When will you do it? This is not the same thing as your 30-60-90 Day Action Plan—that's for your organization. This plan is for **YOU**.

Remember:

Start with simple steps like developing a Job Description for yourself, or having your people fill out the Employee Feedback tool. If you choose something more ambiguous or personal (like, *become a better listener*) then describe it in specific terms that are actionable (*...the next time we have our production meeting I will ask meaningful questions, and listen without interruption*).

Don't forget your calendar! Nothing happens without a deadline, especially in a small, fast-paced environment like a Micro-Organization. Put a date on every item, and work to make it happen.

Be reasonable with your expectations. You're already getting a lot of stuff right. You don't need to change too much all at once. The point is to make a start.

One final comment: Even positive changes can make people uncomfortable. Be prepared for some resistance even to small improvements; be patient with questions and concerns. But don't be deterred from your plan either.

Use DAM Leadership as a compass, providing direction, not all the answers.

As a leader, I will...

1. ____

2. ____

3. ____

4. ____

5. ____

6. ____

7. ____